Who Are the
AMISH?

Who Are the
AMISH?

Merle Good

The People's Place
with

Good Books
Intercourse, Pennsylvania 17534

Photograph Credits

Jerry Irwin: cover photo, 2, 5, 7, 41, 127; Kenneth Pellman: back cover, 8, 10, 15, 17, 18, 20 (top), 33 (top), 33 (bottom), 34 (left), 34 (right), 35, 42 (top), 44 (bottom), 48, 50, 54 (bottom left), 54 (bottom right), 57, 60 (top left), 60 (top right), 60 (bottom), 61, 64 (top), 64 (bottom), 65, 70 (bottom), 81, 82 (top), 84 (bottom), 85 (bottom), 92 (top), 92 (bottom), 94 (bottom left), 94 (bottom right), 95, 100, 101, 102 (top), 102 (bottom), 107, 111 (top), 113, 114 (bottom), 120 (bottom), 122 (top), 122 (bottom), 123 (bottom), 125; Fred Wilson: 11 (top), 11 (bottom), 12, 13, 14 (top), 14, (bottom), 21 (bottom), 23, 44 (top), 52 (top), 52 (bottom), 83 (top), 68, 70 (top), 72, 73, 74, 75 (top), 78, 82 (bottom), 85 (top), 97, 98, 103, 104 (top), 104 (bottom), 105, 110, 111 (bottom), 114 (top); Richard Reinhold: 20 (bottom), 21 (top), 22, 24 (bottom), 32, 45, 63, 75 (bottom), 83, 87, 93 (bottom), 94 (top), 112, 115, 118, 120 (top), 123 (top); David Lauver: 34 (top), 38, 43, 67, 80 (top), 80 (bottom), 93 (top), 108, 121, 124 (bottom); Blair Seitz: 25, 27, 28, 30, 31, 37, 40, 42 (bottom), 51, 53 (bottom), 54 (top), 55, 71, 77, 88, 90, 91, 117, 124 (top); Jonathan Charles: 47; Jan Gleysteen: 58; Merle Good: 62; Steve Scott: 84 (top).

WHO ARE THE AMISH?

Copyright ©1985 by Good Books, Intercourse, PA 17534
International Standard Book Number (hardback): 0-934672-28-8
International Standard Book Number (paperback): 0-934672-26-1
Library of Congress Catalog Card Number: 85-70283

Contents

Another World

Scattered in clusters throughout 22 states and one Canadian province, approximately 135,000 adults and children live the Amish way.

Today there are twice as many Amish persons as there were two decades ago. The Old Order Amish are not fading from the earth. Indeed, by all measurements, this is not a static culture. The Amish communities are, instead, lively and dynamic.

A Distinctive People

A visitor to an Amish community will first notice the obvious differences from the larger American society. The Amish do not own or drive cars; they use horse-drawn buggies instead. They adhere to a distinctive dress style which emphasizes modesty and simplicity. They do not use electricity from public utilities. They prefer farming as a vocation above all others.

But a deeper study reveals more differences and tensions with the larger society. A different view of education has resulted in the one-room Amish school in most communities. A firm belief that the Bible teaches Christians to care for their aging parents has resulted in extended families rather than retirement homes. The same principle has led the Amish to seek exemption from the Social Security system, not because they don't want to pay the tax, but because they are opposed to accepting the benefits. They are very cautious about receiving money from the government for any reason.

For several centuries, the Amish as a group have probably been more consistent than any other group in their opposition to participation in warfare. Their Christian faith leads them to believe, like their Mennonite cousins and other "historic peace churches" such as the Church of the Brethren and the Society of Friends, that they cannot participate in the taking of human life in any situation.

Even time is turned upside down in the Amish community. There is much waiting. A life with no television, no radio, no tele-

The barnraising has become, with good reason, one of the central symbols of Amish society. Working together, building a sturdy, useful, even handsome structure out of the ashes, this activity leaves no doubt about the security of the Amish community.

phone, and no stereos results in waiting for the mail (letters are a prime form of communication), waiting for the bus (many use public transportation for travel when a horse and buggy isn't possible or practical), and waiting for the harvest (use of horse-drawn equipment means less efficiency, on one hand, and a higher risk of rain spoiling the hay or corn harvest, on the other).

A Diverse People

Not all Amish do everything the same way. These people are not museum pieces, stamped out by some identical cookie cutter! They are persons with feelings and personalities the same as humans everywhere.

To say that "the Amish all do this" or "they never do that" is not only grossly inaccurate and unfair; such statements create a zoo. This can be the sad result when these people become the object of blatant commercial tourism. It is also possible for sociologists and other scholars, eager to improve their own careers, to force these people into categories and abnormal "control groups."

The Amish practice a great deal of uniformity in any given church district, but their unity would be shattered quickly if there were no diversity and flexibility between groups and communities. Nearly 100 different horse-drawn vehicles are used by Amish groups. Dress patterns among the Amish are many. How homes are furnished varies a great deal. The list of varieties continues—wedding and courtship practices, the alternate uses of energy, the many non-farming occupations, and even practices of excommunication.

Yet the Amish cohesiveness remains strong. That ability to remain persons, within the structure of a communal society, provides for many a place of security and contented fulfillment.

An Imperfect People

It is possible, upon first learning about the Amish way, to assign all sorts of expectations to these people, to decide that the Amish world is an enchanting paradise, breathlessly idyllic, to believe that it's "splendid and fascinating that the world still has such good people!"

But when an inconsistency appears, that myth of perfection collapses. Then it is possible to decide that everything related to Amish life has a dark edge, a bizarre oppressiveness, a backwardness.

The Amish do not believe that they are perfect. Their teaching on humility encourages them to set high standards for themselves but to constantly realize how much they need God's forgiveness.

These people are not trying to be better than other people. Instead, they are attempting to be faithful to their Christian understandings as best they can. And they fail in this pursuit often. Most Amish will be the first to confess this.

A Christian People

These people believe God has called them to a life of faith, dedication, humility and service. It is that belief in God's personal interest in their lives and their communities which holds them together, in spite of many forces which could easily pull them apart.

This truth cannot be overstressed.

Without a strong Christian conviction about the sacredness and seriousness of life, these people, as a people, would have disappeared a long time ago.

Many who leave the Amish do so to join more evangelical groups. They often question the genuineness of Amish Christianity because many Amish are less verbal about their beliefs than some other Christians for whom "talking" about faith is paramount. These criticisms perhaps miss the point. When one's values are so fully expressed in how one lives, to talk excessively about beliefs seems prideful to Amish believers.

One need not romanticize to suggest that the strengths of Amish society must far outweigh the weaknesses, if one is to believe the evidence. These are not fly-by-night communes, here today, gone tomorrow. This endeavor has continued for centuries, and that requires a central faith, courage, and discipline, and a wonderfulness which overcomes the world.

Journalists, and visitors in general, tend to romanticize the Amish way as an enchanting paradise, breathlessly idyllic, until inconsistencies are discovered. Then words like "bizarre," "oppressive," and "backward" are employed.

The Amish consciously draw limitations for their way of life. Horse-drawn equipment and windmills set a slower pace, closer to nature. And travelling by buggy limits the speed and distance of one's endeavors.

Few images capture the essence of Amish life as well as the quilt: many pieces in one, a thing of beauty which has a utilitarian use, a recycling of old scraps into a new bedcover, and a communal activity which encourages visiting, support, and craftsmanship.

Most Amish communities have horse auctions. But these sales are more than a place to buy and sell. Auctions are educational as fathers teach sons how to judge horses. And best of all it is recreation, a change of scene, and visiting.

With few exceptions, Old Order Amish do not have church buildings. Worship services are held in the homes. Houses are built so that the rooms can be opened up to accommodate the congregation. Church benches (above), owned by the district, are carried into the house in preparation for Sunday services at this Ohio home.

Understanding the Amish is not easy. Most modern Americans are so severely handicapped by the rush of their lives that they find comprehending the Amish people and their way of life and faith virtually impossible.

This is truly another world. One need not find it strange and frightening. Many discover its warmth and precious strength.

The Amish way represents one of the most unusual alternatives to modern society. There is no other explanation why so many tens of thousands stay, why in fact the communities are growing and thriving, and why the whole world, it seems, has turned aside to study the witness of their lives.

Faith and Fields

Few feelings run deeper than a love of the soil. This attachment is not unique to Amish farmers, but it would be a misstatement to suggest that the Amish do not experience an unusual bond with nature.

God of Nature

The Amish believe that the same God who created the world and everything in it also expects his children to be good stewards of that creation. The earth is a sacred trust. Caring for nature requires hard work, sweat, good management, and a respect for the soil.

For the Amish preacher, the Bible bursts with images and parables of nature. After God created the world, he enjoyed it. He called it good. As a climax, God created human beings whom he commanded to harness and cultivate the good earth.

There are different kinds of soils, according to the Bible, each with its own potential, some more conducive to good seed, some more encouraging to weeds. The Amish also believe that dependency on weather teaches dependency on God. There is no bird or flower which escapes the attention of the Creator.

Nature teaches constancy in hardship. Even though the crops fail one year, the soil holds out promise of another harvest. "While the earth remains, seedtime and harvest, cold and heat, summer and winter, and day and night shall not cease."

The Amish do not worship nature. But they do believe that it is easier to be a Christian in a rural setting, close to the parables of nature.

The two most important lessons learned from nature and the soil, perhaps, are central to the faith of these people. First, one learns that a seed, placed into the earth, must die before it can give birth. The images of death and resurrection surround the farmer. And secondly, one keeps learning that, sooner or later, one reaps what one sows.

Farming is a family project. The size of the operation is limited by the ability of the extended family who lives on the farm to handle the work on a year-round calendar. Women help in the fields, and men help in the gardens.

The Amish Farm

The Amish are known as some of the world's best farmers. Part of this arises from their selection of farmlands for settlement.

But a great deal of the success of Amish farms has to do with other factors. Farming for the Amish is not a way to make a fortune so one can retire early and travel around the world. Farming is a way of life. Most Amish pity persons who cannot live on or near farmlands.

Work is both enjoyable and fulfilling. These people view industriousness as an honor to God. And farms need good management. Consequently, both hard work and careful planning are factors.

It is rare that an Amish family will sell their land to a non-Amish buyer. This fact underlines yet another reason for the success of Amish farms—stability. Land is not bought for speculation; it is purchased forever. Therefore there is no pressure to pay off the mortgage in a short span of years. If it takes three generations to clear the mortgage, what does it matter? The farm is in the family to stay! Another factor contributing to the stability of ownership of these farms is the nonexistence of divorce among the Amish (in a few rare instances, Amish couples have separated, but divorce is unheard of).

Rhythms of Nature, Rhythms of Life

The sun is more of a clock for the Amish farmer than for most Americans. During the main growing season, work begins before sunrise and continues until after sunset.

Amish farms are diversified. Seldom does an Amish family put all its eggs in one basket or in one crop. Diversification tends to spread the work around the calendar. Raising only potatoes, for instance, puts more stress on a few short weeks of harvest than a one-row, horse-drawn operation can handle. So the work calendar of the Amish farm tends to be tailored to the plentiful labor of large families and the basic lack of mechanization of their farms.

Dairy herds are very popular as a means of earning significant cash from a relatively small acreage (most Amish farms in Pennsylvania average between 60 and 80 acres; farms among the midwestern Amish tend to be larger, but are still much smaller than the huge acreage of midwestern farms in general). Corn and alfalfa are favorite crops.

In Lancaster County, many Amish farmers raise tobacco as a cash crop; Amish in most other areas frown on this practice (although a fair number of Amish men throughout North America do smoke, especially cigars). The incentive to farm tobacco is that, more than any other crop, tobacco provides work in all four seasons, both young and old can help, and one family can manage it by themselves.

The Amish farmer nourishes the soil. If one's children and grandchildren are to farm the same fields, then the earth must be enriched, not exploited. Good farming methods of crop rotation and fertilizing the soil have long been practiced among the Amish.

The Amish Garden

Food, as noted in later chapters, is central to most festive occasions among the Amish. Gardens dominate a large patch near the house. The special Amish tie to the soil blossoms in the garden as much as in the fields.

Food is not a part of these people's religion. But the preservation and preparation of good healthy food, grown as much as possible on one's own soil, certainly remains a central activity in Amish families.

Non-Farm Occupations

The majority of Amish families earn their living by farming. More and more Amish, however, are by necessity entering farm-related jobs, beginning small cottage industries on or near the farm, or taking up a trade in construction or craftmanship which requires little formal education. Farm life, however, remains central to the Amish way of life.

The two most important lessons learned from nature and the soil, perhaps, are central to the faith of these people. First, one learns that a seed, placed into the earth, must die before it can give birth. The images of death and resurrection surround the farmer. And secondly, one keeps learning that one reaps what one sows.

Nature teaches constancy in hardship. Even though the crops fail one year, the soil holds out promise of another harvest. "While the earth remains, seedtime and harvest, cold and heat, summer and winter, and day and night shall not cease."

The Amish favor growing everything that's possible in the climate in which they live (almost exclusively the temperate zone). This self-sufficiency is displayed especially in the large garden, but also in other food-related projects such as a small orchard, some beehives, or a small handful of chickens, a cow, or a goat.

Beauty expresses itself in spite of the austerity of the Amish way. Flower gardens are popular in most settlements. Many Amish lanes, yards, and fencerows bloom with the most colorful of flowers.

The Amish farmer nourishes the soil. If one's children and grandchildren are to farm the same fields, then the earth must be enriched, not exploited. Good farming methods of crop rotation and fertilizing the soil have long been practiced among the Amish.

Most social activities take place close to home, the fields, and nature. A walk down the lane is a common method of visiting in a world with no telephones, no radio, and no television. The natural sounds and smells permeate even social activities.

The Amish School

How does a child learn? How does a human being of any culture acquire wisdom? If one values the communal life and faith of Amish society, how does one prepare one's children to become contented, productive, fulfilled members of that way of life?

Learning and Wisdom.

A focus on such questions may lead to answers different than those by advocates of modern education. To understand Amish schools and the role of a child in the Amish community, however, these are fair questions. (It is interesting to note that, in recent years, many leading educators are beginning to stress values similar to those embraced by Amish education.)

The Amish are not against education as such. They are cautious, however, about the influence and tone of the so-called "progressive" education of large consolidated schools. Learning and wisdom are important values.

In 1972, the United States Supreme Court granted the Amish and related groups the right to limit formal education to eighth grade. The Amish do not believe in going to court to settle problems, but a committee of concerned persons pursued the case on behalf of the Amish parents who had been arrested for refusing to send their children to high school.

Supreme Court Opinion

"Amish objection to formal education beyond the eighth grade is firmly grounded in central religious beliefs," wrote Chief Justice Warren Burger. "They object to the high school and higher education generally because the values it teaches are in marked variance with Amish values and intellectual and scientific accomplishments, self-distinction, competitiveness, worldly success, and social life with other students.

"Amish society emphasizes informal learning-through-doing, a life of goodness, rather than a life of intellect; wisdom, rather than technical knowledge; community welfare, rather than competition; and separation, rather than integration with contemporary worldly society."

The Amish are not against education as such. They are cautious about the influence and tone of the so-called "progressive" education of large consolidated schools.

In contrast to many religious groups who maintain private schools, the Amish do not teach religion in their schools. Each morning the Bible is read and the Lord's Prayer is repeated in unison. But these people believe that Bible instruction and religious interpretation properly belong only in the church and the home.

In All of Life

However, the Amish hold that how one lives is as important as what one believes. In this respect, religion is fostered all day long.

One Amish school teacher summarized this principle this way: "In arithmetic, by accuracy and no cheating; in English, by learning to say what we mean; in history, by humanity; in health, by teaching cleanliness and thriftiness; in geography, by learning to make an honest living from the soil; in music, by singing praises to God; on the school grounds, by teaching honesty, respect, sincerity, humility, and the Golden Rule."

Most Amish children today attend Amish schools; some in more rural areas continue to attend public schools. Before the 1930s, however, all Amish children attended public schools. The Amish school today in many ways closely resembles the rural one-room school of fifty years ago. Amish schools came into being in direct proportion to the consolidation of public schools.

How Schools Operate

Most Amish schools today have one room and one teacher for all eight grades. Most students walk to school, carrying their lunch boxes (in wintertime the school stove helps to heat potatoes, hot dogs, pizza, sandwiches, soup, or leftovers). English is the language of instruction.

Subjects consist of basic reading, writing and arithmetic. Younger children learn by listening to the older pupils recite their lessons. Older children learn to help the younger. Helping and respecting others is as much a part of education as arithmetic. The Amish schools do meet state standards concerning the number of days and the length of school days.

Teachers are often young Amish women who have not yet married, though it is not unusual to find single women who have taught for many years. Seldom do the teachers themselves have more than eight grades of formal education. Many Amish communities have organized teachers' meetings where more experienced teachers help to train the new ones.

Occasionally the teacher will be a non-Amish person who is trusted by the parents. Sometimes a married Amish man will teach, but it is rare to find a married Amish woman with children at home serving as a regular teacher (the community doesn't want to ask her to leave her home and children).

Teaching materials have been selected and developed by Amish leaders. An Amish publisher in Ontario has developed *Blackboard Bulletin*, a monthly magazine for teachers, and the Old Order Book Society has helped to find wholesome teaching materials.

Parents Are Involved

Parents help to clean the school at the end of the summer. They often visit school unannounced, to show their support of the teacher and the students. Parents volunteer to help the teacher as needed. And they are especially supportive of special school events such as the school Christmas program, the annual school singing, and the end-of-year school picnic (fathers often play ball with the "scholars").

Amish schools are supervised by school boards elected by the parents. Board meetings are generally held monthly to deal with needs, concerns, and problems. The schools are supported by either a school tax approach or a free-will offering.

Generally Successful

The Amish school is not as "backward" as is often supposed. It has generally been successful in preparing young people to be honest, hardworking and conscientious adults, capable of earning a living, raising a Christian family, and contributing to the Amish community.

Most Amish schools today have one room and one teacher for all eight grades. Younger children learn by listening to the older, and the older learn to help the younger. Helping and respecting others is as much a part of education as arithmetic.

The Amish do not teach religion in their schools. Each morning the Bible is read and the Lord's Prayer is repeated in unison. But these people believe that Bible instruction and religious interpretation properly belong only in the church and the home.

The end-of-year school picnic is one of the highlights of the school year. Often fathers play a game of ball with the "scholars." The support of parents for the school is evident in many ways.

The Amish school today closely resembles the rural one-room school of fifty years ago. Teachers are often young, single Amish women, although there are numerous examples of older single women who have taught for many years.

Chief Justice Warren Burger observed: "Amish society emphasizes informal learning-through-doing, a life of goodness, rather than a life of intellect; wisdom, rather than technical knowledge; community welfare, rather than competition; and separation, rather than integration with contemporary worldly society."

The Amish school has, in general, been successful in preparing young people to be honest, hardworking, and conscientious adults, capable of earning a living, raising a Christian family, and contributing to the Amish community.

Seasons of Life

The rhythms of nature have many parallels in the seasons of Amish life.

Childhood

Children are cherished among the Amish. Most families are large, and children are viewed as "a gift from the Lord."

Many babies are born at home, but hospitals are used too. In some communities, doctors have established birthing rooms.

An Amish baby is not baptized upon birth because the Amish practice adult believer's baptism. They believe God loves all children and protects them in their innocence.

Relatives and friends flock to visit the new baby. Small practical presents, often food or clothing, may be shared. The Amish have traditionally favored the use of biblical names such as Joseph, John, Rebecca, and Sarah, but, in the Midwest especially, this practice is breaking down.

Children learn many skills—how to bake bread, how to plant a crop, how to care for animals, how to speak and write two different languages (the Amish speak English and the Pennsylvania German dialect and they learn to read and write both English and standard German), how to live without electricity, and how to be an individual and still submit to the wishes of one's Amish community.

Children feel needed, wanted, and loved. Working hard is fulfilling when it serves a purpose. And not all of life is work. Plenty of time is found for picnics, fishing, cornerball, and visiting. Toys are mostly homemade. This necessity to innovate encourages creativity.

Courtship

One of the main social activities for Amish young people is the Singing. Practices vary from community to community, but generally several hundred unmarried young people may attend a Singing.

Growing up Amish certainly has its sense of limitations. But this must be seen in the context of a sense of belonging. Everyone feels needed. Children are loved and encouraged in their individuality. Surrounded by security, clear expectations, structures and role models, these children experience a sense of hope and belonging that is rare in today's world.

The tempo of the music sung may move faster and be more contemporary than the slow unison chant of Sunday church.

Afterwards, at the more lively gatherings, guitars, fiddles, banjos and harmonicas may be used. In some communities, square dancing sometimes climaxes the evening, though this is not sanctioned by parents.

Courtship becomes, for many Amish young people, one of the favorite seasons of their lives. Love is instilled as a commitment, a loyal friendship to a mate, intertwined with affection and feeling.

The young man normally takes the initiative. Who is dating whom remains somewhat secretive, though generally parents are quite aware of the courtship. Amish marriages are not arranged, but courtship takes place within the framework of clear expectations.

Weddings

Amish young people traditionally do not have an extended engagement period before marriage. Public announcement of the intention to marry is normally made several weeks before the wedding by the deacon or the bishop. Most weddings take place after the harvest is finished, in November and December.

The wedding day begins as early as 5 a.m. and continues until late at night. Relatives, friends and members of the church district are invited in person or by postcard. In Lancaster County, weddings are normally held on Tuesdays and Thursdays.

Guests begin arriving before dawn; they are greeted by a handshake from the bride and groom. The bride has made her own wedding dress (and often supplies material for the dresses of her two attendants). White is not used; dark colors are preferred (navy, dark blue, or purple are usual in Lancaster County). The groom and his attendants wear the traditional white shirt, black suit, black shoes, and black felt hat.

The wedding service closely parallels a regular church service in many aspects: three or four hours in length with scripture reading, two sermons, and much singing. But there are unique features. The service starts with male relatives of the groom be-

ginning traditional wedding hymns from the *Ausbund* (as usual, the "Loblied" is the second hymn) while the bride and the groom meet upstairs with the bishop and ministers who question them on their understanding of the seriousness of faith and marriage. Marriage is for life; divorce is not an option.

Then the bride and groom, ushered by their attendants, take their place near the ministers' row, the three young men facing the three young women.

The sermon includes stories of marriage from the Bible, from Adam and Eve to the Apocrypha. The bishop asks the couple to stand, asks them to answer three questions, and has a special prayer with them. Then they return to their seats for the concluding half hour of the service.

The remainder of the day is spent in feasting, singing and visiting. Many times guests will leave in the afternoon and go to another wedding, while others arrive from yet another wedding! Wedding season marks the high point of Amish social life.

In many communities, the newly married couple will not take up housekeeping until late winter or spring. They will spend long weekends together and an occasional week or two. The groom's family generally takes responsibility to help the new couple get established financially.

Family Life

Wedding time is followed by the season of bearing children and getting a start financially. Child rearing suddenly becomes the most important responsibility of the young couple. No other expression of love and one's faith surpasses the care and nurturing of one's children.

Retirement

Retirement comes early. This purposeful decision gives the younger generation a greater sense of ownership in the family farm or the business. As an Amish adult moves toward the autumn of life, working with one's hands, learned as a child, becomes the source of enjoyment again.

The seasons of Amish life create a full circle.

Courtship becomes, for many Amish young people, one of the favorite seasons of their lives. Love is instilled as a commitment, a loyal friendship to a mate, intertwined with affection and feeling. Marriage is for life; divorce is not an option among the Amish.

A wedding scene in Lancaster County, Pennsylvania. Hundreds of guests attend the happy event which begins before dawn, includes a service of more than three hours, a large wedding feast, fellowship and singing, a wedding supper, and singing late into the evening. Notice the porch has been enclosed to make more space inside the house, a common practice.

Working hard is part of being an Amish adult. But work is enjoyable and meaningful if one does it for those one loves. Laboring side by side with extended family and hand in hand with nature can generate pleasure, whether it's picking strawberries at dawn or making hay at sunset.

Wedding time is followed by the season of bearing children and getting a start financially. Raising a family becomes the most important responsibility of a young Amish couple. No other expression of love and one's faith surpasses the care and nurturing of one's children.

BARBARA DAU of
SAMUEL & FANNY
STOLTZFOOS
DIED OCT. 26th 1881
AGED 50 YRS
8 MO 24 DYS

Death

Death is as expected as birth for these people. It's only natural, the Amish believe, the way God meant life to be.

Death in community is normally not as lonely and devastating as it is in modern, "progressive" society. The bereaved are surrounded by family and friends. They're given help with the farm work, food, and time with the children who have lost their parent or grandparent.

Silence dominates the mood as family and friends come to view the deceased and sit with the bereaved. Even the funeral and the burial are quiet. The funeral follows the form of a regular service, but hymns are spoken instead of sung.

Life is brief, the Amish are reminded. Those who live to see the beauty of autumn should be grateful. But winter is not frightening. It too is a natural part of the seasons of life.

A line of buggies proceeds up the hill, bearing the deceased to a final resting place in an Amish graveyard. In death, as in birth and in all of life, the Amish individual is surrounded by the community of faith. These people live by the words of the biblical poet, "To everything there is a season."

Belonging Together

In a culture dominated by the ideal of individual freedom, most Americans spend little time developing the belonging part of themselves. The modern credo seems to say that to be "mature" one must be free of ties to others, uninvolved, uncommitted, and unencumbered.

In such a setting, the Amish world seems like a foreign country. And it is.

Children

In many ways Amish life is structured around children and family life. At first glance, Amish children may appear to lead restricted lives, cut off from the opportunity to fulfill their individual destinies. Most homes observe firm patterns of discipline. A child is surrounded by expectations, and that can seem a burden.

On the other hand, few children in our world today lead as contented, fulfilled lives as most Amish children do, surrounded by security, clear expectations and structures, numerous role models both inside and outside of their own extended families, and a sense of hope and belonging. More isolated than most children, yes. More deprived, hardly. More prepared to be a scientist or astronaut, no. More prepared to make a contribution to Amish society, yes.

It's the belonging part of a child which goes underdeveloped in the larger world. But with the Amish, identity begins in knowing where and to whom one belongs.

Doesn't Just Happen

But a sense of community doesn't just fall out of the clouds. It requires purposeful planning, the Amish believe, just like a crop. Belonging together calls for planting, watering, cultivation and weeding, and a willingness to help to reap the harvest, regardless of the climate.

For most Amish, the belonging together is a way of life. Every decision is not con-

The kitchen table is central in Amish homes. Here's where meals are taken. Here's where large work projects are done together, whether baking, canning and preserving, or even farm bookkeeping and planning. Here's where the family gathers, night after night, a single lamp hung from the ceiling as family members sew, read, crayon, tell stories and visit. The farmstead is dark and the whole family ends the day together.

stantly debated. But the fact that many Amish may not be able to explain why they live as they do or to give a detailed rationale for various practices and rules does not mean that Amish leadership has not thought it through. Careful, deliberate leadership over many generations has undergirded the Amish cohesiveness.

Leadership

The selection of leadership for the Old Order Amish combines democracy and faith. The church district comprises the central unit of authority and peoplehood. Districts are usually measured in size by the number of families instead of the number of persons. When there are more persons at Sunday service than can be conveniently accommodated in their homes, a district will divide into two new districts.

The most influential person in the district is normally the bishop. His authority is immense. He holds final word on all matters of faith and practice. Each male and female member has a vote on matters brought before the congregation, but the opinion of the bishop has definite sway.

The Amish practice a "three-fold ministry": 1) the bishop, who is the chief shepherd of the congregation, performs marriages, baptisms, excommunication and funerals and leads out in matters of faith and life: 2) the ministers, normally two, who carry key responsibility for preaching and counselling; and 3) the deacon, whose main responsibility relates to material aid within the congregation, but who also plays a key role in maintaining church discipline as well as the usually delightful function in marriage arrangements.

All three of these positions are filled in a two-step process. After much preaching and prayer, and after receiving affirmative counsel from the congregation, opportunity is given for all members to nominate a brother from their congregation for the position. Usually more than one vote is needed, and usually there are numerous nominees. The lot is then used to select from this group of nominees. The Amish believe that God reveals to them through this process who their leader should be.

Amish leaders carry their authority in a wide variety of manners. When the leader is heavyhanded, there is often resistance. An effective leader learns to be compassionate, flexible, but firm.

The district has final authority in matters of church polity and discipline. There is no sense of "denominational hierarchy" among the Amish. In some areas, bishops do meet to confer informally on a regular basis. (Each church district decides with which other districts they will fellowship and share communion.)

"Ordnung"

Most aspects of an Amish person's life are governed by rules and regulations known as *Ordnung*. These have evolved over many years, are normally not written down, and are further clarified, developed or modified at special meetings before communion twice a year. But *Ordnung* is not set in concrete. These are dynamic communities of faith, and the flexibility of their mutual understandings provides a key to their healthy growth.

Social Activities Aplenty

What holds these people together and nurtures their sense of belonging? Certainly, their faith in God does. The worship service is central. Strong grassroots leadership is another factor. A detailed set of rules and regulations help. And a common identity in language, food, architecture, music, vocation, dress, transportation, schooling, and witness all contribute.

But the role of visiting should not be underestimated. This art, largely lost in the dominant American culture, supplies the rich fabric of Amish togetherness. The Amish spend a great deal of time each week dropping in on other families, catching up on the latest news and concerns.

And the special occasions and the belonging become a delight. Quiltings are great for visiting; so are auctions and barn-raisings. "Sisters day" brings extended family together. Birthday parties, homemade ice cream and pie, 'and picnics all strengthen the bonds.

Few groups in America work so hard at developing a sense of belonging.

The worship service, every other week, remains the single most important unity of the Amish. It is considered prideful for an Amishman to seek the ministry. The responsibility is a heavy load. But if the congregation and God together call one to lead, then it is prideful to refuse the unwanted task.

Three generations, and sometimes even four, often work together. But the Amish extended family differs from some other cultures. The grandparents have their own home, built onto or next to the main house. And the grandparents take their meals in their own quarters, not around a big table for all generations. The ideal is to let the parents of growing children function as parents, independent as much as possible from the meddling of the grandparents.

The art of visiting builds a reinforcement and unity in the fabric of Amish society. Whether it's a barnraising (below), an auction (above), a quilting, meeting at the store, waiting for the bus, or stopping to see the new baby, visiting happens constantly.

Perhaps the widespread fascination with the Amish way is truly a question of identity. Millions of Americans turn aside to ask themselves, "To whom do I belong?" and "Could I be so much in charge of my life, so committed, so willing to go against the tide for my beliefs?"

Home is a theme central to the Amish communities. Home, the place of birth, and probably the place of death. Home is where church happens, weddings, baptisms, birthday get-togethers, and funerals. The only Amish institution outside the home is the school. Even the printing press, the mutual aid office, and the historical library reside at the homeplace.

Everything prepares for night. One can hear the birds, the insects, the wind in the grass, the breathing of the horse. As one buggy owner said, "*You* might get there faster, but I hear and see more along the way."

Tradition and History

The Amish are a small group, numbering a total population of about 135,000 in North America, of whom approximately half are baptized members. While 75% of the Old Order Amish live in the three states of Ohio, Pennsylvania, and Indiana, there are numerous settlements scattered across 19 other states and Ontario. Although they originated in Europe, there are no settlements remaining there, and attempts to plant Old Order Amish communities in Central and South America have not been successful.

Sense of Martyrdom

One of the great ironies of the Amish people is the tension between their sense of settledness and their feeling of being a persecuted people. Though a given farmer may be tilling soil which six or seven generations of his ancestors cultivated before him, he lives with a resignation within himself that "Any day now, we may have to move on again, because the world sees us as an enemy."

This sense of martyrdom may seem shocking to observers. It arises partly from the tensions Amish society experiences constantly with the larger American culture. But to a larger degree, it originates in the history and the religious literature of these people.

Beginnings

The Amish and the Mennonites are like religious cousins. They are Christians who date their roots back to the Anabaptist movement of the early 1500s in Switzerland. (The nickname "Anabaptist" means "rebaptizer.")

At the same time, Martin Luther and Ulrich Zwingli were beginning their break with the church in Rome. The Anabaptists called themselves simply "Brethren" and

This cave in the Swiss mountains became a refuge for Anabaptists during the sixteenth century. The Amish trace their roots to these radical Christians who believed that the church should be a group of adults, baptized upon voluntary confession of faith, and like the early Christians, separated from both the world and the state.

are often referred to by historians as the Radical Reformation. They were active in Switzerland, Germany, and the Netherlands.

They became severely persecuted by both the church of Rome and the Reformers, because they represented a third option: a belief that the church should be a group of adults, baptized upon voluntary confession of faith, and like the early Christian Church, separated from both the world and the state.

The movement spread quickly and the Anabaptists were put to death by the thousands. Many of the leaders were dead within a few years. What began among educated urban radicals became a rural peasant movement as the believers fled to the caves and mountains.

One leader who helped hold together the fragmented survivors was Menno Simons, a Dutch priest from Friesland, who himself left the Catholic church in 1536 after years of struggle. His group was nicknamed "Mennoists" and later "Mennonites."

Jacob Amman

The Amish began as a group, however, 150 years after the Reformation in 1693 when a young Swiss Mennonite elder from the Alsace, who felt the church was losing its purity, broke with his brethren and formed a new Christian fellowship.

His name was Jacob Amman and his followers were nicknamed "Amish." Their debate focused on a difficult question: "If a member is excommunicated from the fellowship, how severe should the discipline be?" Other issues such as communion, feetwashing, and beards were involved, but the central issue was the renewal of the church.

Several attempts to heal the division failed. It remains an important issue for the Amish today. If one believes that the church consists of adults who voluntarily commit themselves to the fellowship and discipline of their fellow believers, then the purity of the church becomes very important. Otherwise the core collapses and the commitment becomes fickle.

The Amish have suffered numerous divisions since their beginnings. Personality conflicts have contributed. But almost always the central concern has involved the purity and faithfulness of the fellowship.

Migrations

Several hundred Amish migrated to Pennsylvania from Switzerland and the German Palatinate during the first half of the 1700s. They fled religious persecution in Europe and were delighted by William Penn's hospitality. But becoming landowners, relating to the Indians, and remaining conscientious objectors in the Revolutionary War all threatened Amish cohesiveness. Early on in America, Amish leaders learned that when persecution no longer holds their people together, prosperity and social freedom can disintegrate a group. A second wave of migration took place between 1815 and 1860 primarily from the Alsace; most of these Amish settled further west.

The Bible

The Bible remains the central book of the Amish people. Because the average Amish adult does not read contemporary English versions of the Bible or participate in modern interpret-for-yourself Bible study groups, some Christian groups picture the Amish as unconcerned about the Bible and its teachings. This is both unfair and untrue.

The Amish view the Bible as the guide for faith and life. Over the centuries they have together developed statements and understandings based on Scripture. These are further detailed in the rules and regulations of each district, governing not just one's activities, but also one's attitudes (humility, forgiveness, etc.). But the Amish believe that the whole framework is based on the Bible.

The German Bible plays a central role in the Amish worship service. Read by the deacon before the main sermon, quoted at length by the preachers during the two sermons, and read again after the main sermon, the average Amish person hears a great deal of Scripture.

In most Amish homes today, a book which records years of persecution, called *The Martyrs Mirror*, plays an important function in reminding these people of the sufferings of their ancestors. In many ways it undergirds their belief that the world is not to be fully trusted.

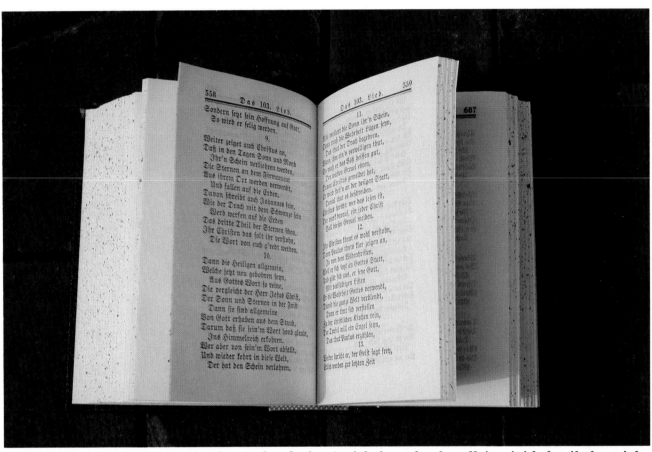

Even many of the hymns in the *Ausbund*, the Amish hymnbook, tell in vivid detail the trials, tortures, and faithfulness of martyrs long ago. Also found in most Amish homes is the prayerbook *Christenpflicht*. To pray aloud spontaneously seems insincere to many Amish.

It is fascinating to notice parallels between practices among the Amish, historically in Europe, and practices found among the Amish, today—dress patterns, language, farming methods, music, covered bridges (in Europe, above; near Lancaster, Pa., right), food, flower gardens and painted designs.

The Old World influences contributed heavily to Amish society in the New World. It would be a gross mistake, however, to view the Amish as a transplanted peasant culture from Europe. The dynamic vitality of these communities defies such offhand categorization.

While an Amish farmer may be tilling the same soil which six or seven generations of his ancestors cultivated before him, he lives with a resignation within himself that, "Any day now, we may have to move on again because the world sees us as an enemy."

Sometimes one must move on with one's family. Maybe it is in search of land. Often it is a matter of conscience, seeking a less frantic place to settle in peace, close to nature, close to family, and close to God. But Amish families do not move to new regions alone; several families will move to the same area so they have enough persons to form a new church district within horse-and-buggy distance of each other.

Interaction with the World

Local Involvements

In most areas, the Amish are active in supporting voluntary community organizations which are related to the general welfare such as fire and emergency services. Volunteer fire companies in towns and hamlets throughout Amish communities often have many crew members who are Amish.

Benefit auctions are sometimes held to raise money for a new ambulance or fire engine. Many Amish not only attend these auctions as buyers; they often heavily donate items such as baked goods, farm equipment or livestock, crafts, and especially quilts, to the auction. Many are active in helping with the food concession and the actual carrying of items to and from the auctioneer's platform. (It is rare to find an Old Order Amish auctioneer.)

Organizations for the blind and handicapped are often supported by the Amish. Many Amish groups cooperate with their Mennonite cousins in two relief organizations.

Relief Organizations

Through Mennonite Central Committee, the Amish participate in supporting relief needs around the globe. This worldwide service agency distributes many millions of dollars of aid and service to countries of all political affiliations, "in the name of Christ."

The Amish become most involved in MCC by making or donating clothing and basics such as soap and bedding; by helping to can meat to be sent around the world to hungry people; and by making quilts, crafts and food to be sold at large public relief sales which may raise several hundred thousand dollars in a single day!

A second relief organization supported by many Amish groups is Mennonite Disaster Service. In time of floods, hurricanes, tornadoes, fires, or other disasters, crews

Some Amish communities are more secluded than others. This accounts for a great variety in the extent of interchange Amish persons experience with the larger world. Buying and selling, in a multitude of ways, is their most common way of interacting with the larger world.

of Mennonites and Amish, volunteering their time, will go to areas throughout North America to help dig out, clean up, or rebuild. Some give a day, some a week, some as long as a year.

This desire to help others expresses itself in many other ways—food to a sick neighbor, help with a widow's farmwork, donations for much-needed surgery. Giving money to help others is a very private matter among the Amish, but is probably more common than is generally supposed.

Personal Interaction

Many visitors may stop by the average Amish farm—salesmen of all sorts, persons to buy milk or eggs, or customers for a small cottage industry operated by the family. Many Amish themselves will shop for a variety of wares at the smaller shopping centers or downtown stores, though the springing up of Amish stores throughout the countryside has lessened this.

These people normally have good relationships with their non-Amish neighbors. Many Amish are reserved but friendly; if one is content with one's identity, persons from other lifestyles are less threatening.

Buying and selling is their most common way of interacting with the larger world. Visiting back and forth between each other's homes is less common. Most Amish people tend to be cautious about inviting non-Amish friends and neighbors to their home for a meal on a regular basis, but many Amish will invite non-Amish for a special occasion. The home (which doubles as the church) is the nest of Amish society, and it is protected as such.

As the Amish population continues to grow rapidly and farmland in general keeps being macadamed, more and more Amish are seeking work away from home. Many Amish leaders consider "the lunch pail" one of the greatest threats to Amish society. Many immigrate to less populous areas. Nonetheless, it is true that an increasing number of Amish persons are working for non-Amish employers.

Relating to Government

The relationship of the Amish communities to local, state, and federal governments may best be described as respectful but wary. In addition to being mindful of their history of persecution by governments in Europe, the Amish also realize that many of their beliefs put them in tension with the desires of governments today.

If members of one's group have gone to prison for adhering to important beliefs, one may be somewhat suspicious of the government. Some Amish groups have experienced intense pressure from government concerning their schools, their opposition to Social Security, various practices related to horse-drawn vehicles, health matters, and peace and nonresistance issues. (Besides, how can governments keep track of people who have no driver's licences, no Social Security numbers and no credit cards!)

The Amish pay all taxes (except where exempt from the Social Security tax). These are law-abiding citizens. Crime rates and unemployment rates in Amish communities tend to be low.

Most Amish do not vote in public elections, are opposed to serving in government in any manner, and are very suspicious of accepting government aid.

Misconceptions

One should not close this discussion without pointing out that perhaps the most common way in which the larger world interacts with the Amish communities is through misconceptions. Because Amish life is so dramatically different from mainstream America, many conclusions are drawn without information or knowledge. Often this turns to ridicule, and even occasionally to violence (as in the case of the Amish baby in Indiana who was killed by an object thrown into a buggy by scornful neighborhood youths passing in a speeding truck).

The Amish do not employ public relations agencies. They see no need to explain their faith and life to a world that is curious but is not willing to truly believe. On one hand, this isolation contributes to misconceptions; on the other hand, the Amish refusal to try to impress the larger culture is a key to their survival.

Benefit auctions are sometimes held to raise money for a new ambulance or fire engine. Many Amish not only attend these auctions as buyers; they often donate heavily to these auctions, items such as baked goods, farm equipment or livestock, crafts, and especially quilts.

An increasing number of cottage industries have sprung up as the Amish population continues to grow. Amish stores dot the countryside, often on the farm, specializing in groceries, yard goods, non-electric hardware, health foods, or furniture.

Many Amish are quite active in a relief agency similar to the Red Cross called Mennonite Disaster Service. They travel many miles to contribute days of free labor to help flood, fire, and hurricane or tornado victims.

Here Amish volunteers help prepare meat to be canned and shipped overseas through Mennonite Central Committee. This worldwide service agency distributes many millions of dollars of aid and service to countries of all political affiliations, "in the name of Christ."

Some Amish children attend public schools where consolidation has been minimal. Here Amish school children are bussed to a public school for a hot lunch. In general, however, Amish children have less interaction with the larger world than their parents do.

Some Amish travel more than others. A visit to the zoo is a fairly common experience. Flower gardens and history museums may be patronized, too. Some Amish young people experiment with a variety of amusements before they join the church, but normally their social life includes mainly Amish neighbors and relatives, as in the skating scene below.

Drawing Lines

Where a group draws its lines is often somewhat arbitrary. They could move one way or another without changing much. Therefore it is the easiest thing in the world to ridicule where someone else has drawn a line. And turning a spotlight on the line can make it appear silly. But the line has a purpose nonetheless.

The Amish understand this.

Tensions with Society

The Amish, as a people of God, feel called to be separate from the world. They believe the Christian way will not be chosen by the majority of society. God's people are a faithful minority. Therefore, nearly everything which is embraced wholeheartedly by the larger American culture is greeted with skepticism by the Old Order Amish.

This clearly leads to tensions and misunderstandings with their neighbors. But these people find courage in remembering that their ancestors in Europe went to prison and even gave their lives for their beliefs.

Upside-Down Purpose

Many children in the larger American society grow up being coached to try "to make it," or "to get some place in life," or "to be somebody."

These ideas are alien to Amish society. There is no place to go; one already has a people. What's the point of "making it" if ostentation is forbidden; how will anyone know one has "made it" if one can't show it off? In any case, the lines have been drawn and the expectations set in such a way that to "be somebody" is to become an humble, responsible, loving member of the Amish community.

This does not mean that Amish persons do not experience ambition, envy, even greed. They are human beings. But the orientation to life is so upside down by

Amish leaders know that the purpose of drawing lines is to define a center. For many, clear boundaries enrich the heart of being a part of a people of God. But for some, those same boundaries become oppressive. That is the hard part of drawing lines.

American standards, that unless this is understood, many of the ways in which the Amish draw lines can seem weird.

Transportation

The Amish have observed that persons who leave the Amish and begin driving cars do, in fact, lose a certain quality in their living. Families are more fragmented; fewer and fewer meals are taken by the family unit as a whole; seldom at eight o'clock in the evening will one find the entire family at home; and visiting among family members happens less and less.

But the bigger problem is what happens in a car owner's head; nothing seems too big or far; a machine the size of an automobile gives its owner a fantasy of power which is unnatural, the Amish say.

In a word, cars separate people more than buggies do, they speed up the tempo of the people's lives, and they warp their owners' sense of self-importance.

The result is nearly 100 different types of horse-drawn vehicles among the Amish today. The average buggy costs $2,000 to $3,000, depending on the style and the community. Horse auctions are common because few Amish raise their own horses.

Weather becomes a major factor in buggy transportation. Some groups forbid the closed-in buggy; some drive top buggies with open fronts; some forbid any top. These require heavy clothes and blankets, an umbrella, and a pioneer spirit.

Amish buggies vary in color; black is the most common. The grey top buggy appears mainly among the Amish of Lancaster County. Smaller groups elsewhere also use yellow top buggies, yellow-brown top buggies, or the white top buggies with a brown box.

Appearance

There is no uniform style of dress among the Amish, although the basic elements are generally the same. Patterns, sizes, and colors of bonnets and hats, for instance, vary a great deal from place to place.

But the principles are uniform. A Christian will look different from the world in his or her appearance, the Amish believe, as do other groups of the Plain People such as the Hutterites, the Old Order River Brethren, and many Mennonite groups.

Once again, it is easy to ridicule where each group draws its lines. But the central concern should not be missed. In a fashion-conscious America, the Amish choose to emphasize separation, simplicity and modesty.

Schools, Mutual Aid, Energy and Aging

Each of these four subjects is treated at length elsewhere. But in a discussion of drawing lines, it is important to notice that the central vision of the Amish people is consistently drawn, in every aspect of life, from cradle to grave. That thoroughness of defining how to be "God's faithful minority" explains in large part the vitality and stability of the Amish communities.

Peace

The Amish are perhaps the most consistent of all groups in adhering almost universally to the conscientious objector stance. This was one of Jacob Amman's concerns in the Amish beginnings in Alsace.

Sometimes farm deferments have been available. In some wars an exemption fee was paid. In more recent wars, large numbers of Amish youths performed alternative service as conscientious objectors in public service or public health projects.

But the principle is firm—the Amish do not wish to take the life of another human being. They have also traditionally been opposed to the use of force in lawsuits or union membership. This refusal to bear arms also has led to a general caution about voting in public elections.

Lines Create a Center

In the end, the purpose of drawing lines is to define a center. And for most of the Amish, clear boundaries have only made the center more precious.

Dress styles vary a great deal. Note the pleats on this woman's cap. Unmarried teenage girls normally wear a white cap during the week and a black cap on Sundays. On her wedding day, the bride wears her black cap for the last time. Note the broad brim (below) of this Nebraska Amish man's hat, his long hair, no suspenders, and the colonial style of his shirt.

This beautiful fraktur by an Amish bishop celebrates the Amish love of peace. These people have consistently, over many centuries, been opposed to participation in warfare. Their belief in Christian peace is yet another line they've drawn which results in tension with the larger culture.

In this Lancaster County community, a local supermarket has developed a store on wheels, visiting the various farms and hamlets. The housewife walks through the truck, completing her shopping in a matter of minutes. But the Amish do go to town, too, to shop, to visit the doctor or the bank, to use the telephone, and to visit.

The contrast between the Amish methods of farming and those of modern farmers highlights the consequences of drawing lines: fewer acres are farmed and in a much more labor-intensive style. Here two teams harvest corn for silo filling while a third team brings the empty wagon.

Notice the variety of colors and shapes in these buggies in a central Pennsylvania community. The Amish believe that cars separate people more than buggies do, cars often speed up the tempo of people's lives, and they tend to warp their owner's sense of self-importance.

The Amish communities are constantly changing and updating their practices. Rules and regulations vary from district to district. While the Amish may appear very unchanging to an outsider, a closer look reveals a great deal of change.

(Note the steel wheels on this hydraulic plow; note also the especially adapted padded seat!)

But sometimes there are disagreements and church splits. Sometimes anger erupts. Sometimes members will move away in the middle of the storm. Not every line that's drawn brings unity.

Sources of Energy

The Amish, more than any other group, continue to believe that various uses of energy and mechanization do threaten the cohesiveness of their Christian community.

But Why?

Many Amish leaders draw the line in defining whether a church district belongs to the Old Order Amish by asserting that, to be an Old Order group, the members must drive horse-drawn buggies instead of cars and must also live without electricity from public utilities (batteries are permitted).

On the use of electricity and modern mechanization, one Amish leader from Indiana put it this way: "We feel it right to lead simple, consistent, and well-ordered lives. However, it is becoming more and more difficult to live simply. We realize and are more or less aware that the more modern equipment we have and the more mechanized we become, the more we are drawn into the swirl of the world, and away from the simplicity of Christ and our life in Him."

Many Americans find this sort of thinking hard to understand. The machine is practically worshipped by moderns as that which has enriched life, opened incredible opportunities, taken man to the moon, and enhanced ease (though most are not sure if life has become more fulfilling).

Take the tractor, for instance. How can the Amish possibly object to the use of an ordinary tractor to do their field work?

An Amishman from Iowa answers, "The tractor in itself does not appear to be anything so bad. But when we look into the history of the Amish churches which have changed and permitted the use of the tractor for field work, we must conclude that it does have a significant influence on the life and thinking of a group.

"Only a few communities have been able to retain their Amish simplicity with the tractor. Dozens have been carried away from the Amish by the tractor!"

The sun remains the most important source of energy for the Amish. Crops need sunshine. An increasing number of uses of solar energy are emerging among the Amish, too, for heating water, providing heat to buildings and greenhouses, and in several cases, energizing the lights on a young man's buggy!

No Electricity?

There is enormous variety in practice among the Amish when it comes to energy sources, uses, and adaptations.

For instance, water is pumped in a whole range of methods: 1) a simple hand pump is required in some communities; 2) the use of the windmill is very common, pumping water to a storage tank (sometimes an upended railroad tank car) where it can then flow down by gravity to the house and barn as needed; 3) waterwheels are used in some communities; a paddle-wheel arrangement in a small stream creates a motion by wire which activates a pump at the well; 4) water rams are used by some for livestock; 5) pneumatic pumps are used increasingly in wells; or 6) a gasoline or diesel motor is used to run the pump.

Milk is cooled in various ways. In Lancaster County, often believed to be one of the more conservative communities, Amish leaders decided that a modern milk tank arrangement required to produce first-grade quality milk was not a threat to their cohesiveness. Dairy operations prosper; milking is done by machine; and diesel engines keep the milk cool in the big tanks.

On the other hand, some communities milk their herds by hand, store their milk in milk cans, keep these cans in a cooler cooled by either cold water or an engine, and ship their milk to cheese plants.

Some groups use only kerosene lamps for lighting; most, however, also use pressurized lamps filled with naphtha or "white gas." Many use these pressurized lamps in their chicken houses to extend the day in wintertime.

Wood stoves are common, as are stoves energized by natural gas or kerosene. In some communities, refrigerators are run by kerosene, in many others by natural gas. Ice boxes are used in some places. Washing machines may be run by hand, by gasoline engine, by hydraulic, or by pneumatic power driven by a gasoline or diesel motor. Irons are heated on the stove or by pressurized gas. Shavers, flashlights, and fruit juicers are often battery operated (as are the flashing lights on buggies).

Tractors are normally restricted to belt power use, such as silo filling. Some groups permit no tractors and use stationary engines for belt power. Many groups permit a tractor with steel wheels (no rubber) to be used on occasion to pull unusually heavy loads. Of course, all of these generalizations have many exceptions.

As noted above, most leaders believe that when an Amish farmer acquires a tractor with rubber tires, he has left the Old Order Amish.

New Order Amish

During the past two decades, there have been an increasing number of New Order Amish groups coming into being. Their characteristics vary a great deal also, but, in general, they are more open to technology. Many of these groups put electricity and telephones in their homes; a lot farm with tractors, but continue to use the horse and buggy for transportation.

The main reasons given by persons who leave the Old Order to join the New Order (it is sometimes done by a whole district at a time) are an interest in having Sunday School, more Bible study, and more "spiritual" activities for their young people. Total population of New Order groups at this writing is approximately 4,500 to 5,000 persons of whom about half are baptized members.

Invention

One of the major side effects of Amish cautions on technology and restrictions on certain energy uses is the continual development of creative ingenuity and invention. New ways to adapt technology but stay within the rules are constantly emerging. A woodworking shop, for instance, may have most modern tools, powered by pneumatic power instead of electricity.

Another opportunity for ingenuity comes with the need to repair the equipment used by the Amish. Much of it is no longer manufactured and no parts are available. Many shops scattered throughout the Amish communities specialize in rebuilding worn-out, out-of-date equipment or in inventing new parts.

The majority of Amish do not permit use of the bicycle. Rubber tires on vehicles, whether tractors, buggies, or bicycles, encourage travelling farther and longer; some communities do use the bicycle, however. In Lancaster County bicycles are not permitted but scooters with rubber tires are increasingly popular.

This young woman is guiding *horses*, pulling a hay baler, driven by *belt power*, supplied by the *gasoline motor*, as the same *sun* which caused the hay to grow, and also dried the hay, provides the daylight for the horses and her to see what they're doing!

Telephones

The problem with telephones is the incoming calls. The Amish home is filled with natural sounds; one can hear birds or the animals at the barn or the grandfather singing in his shop. The absence of television, radio, stereos and incoming telephone calls creates an entirely different atmosphere than one finds in the average American home.

The Amish vary in their use of public telephones. Most communities are dotted with phone booths, often in weather-protected little sheds. The phone is used by most for urgent calls only; otherwise letter-writing suffices. Persons operating a cottage industry at their farm or home may utilize the phone more frequently, but it is still kept outside their buildings. (A loud bell may be attached so an incoming call can be heard.)

Kerosene lamps (above) or pressurized lamps (left) are commonly used for general lighting. Ironically, Amish farmers who do not use electricity may have to put up with massive power lines cutting through their farms. (Another irony—Amish farms in Lancaster County were threatened by the Three Mile Island nuclear accident only twenty miles away!)

In the end, the greatest energy source for the Amish community comes from their togetherness, their commitment, and their faith, whether it's gathering for church, a wedding, a funeral, or a mutual aid meeting. Note the saw (below) driven by pneumatic power, which in turn is driven by a diesel engine.

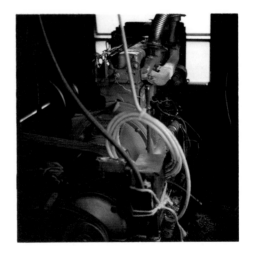

The waterwheel, above, symbolizes a simplicity, a closeness to natural things. "We realize and are more or less aware that the more modern equipment we have and the more mechanized we become," an Amish leader observes, "the more we are drawn into the swirl of the world, and away from the simplicity of Christ and our life in Him."

The Barnraising

The Fire

A barn bursting into flames during the night is a terrible sight. Sometimes lightning strikes in a heavy storm. Sometimes the gasses from freshly-baled green hay get trapped in the barn and erupt into a sheet of fire. Occasionally a malfunctioning motor is the cause. The most tragic instances are those of arson.

In Amish communities, the trauma of the destruction of a farm family's barn is softened by the immediate help and care which surrounds them.

The Amish believe in mutual aid. The Bible urges Christians to "bear one another's burdens," and the Amish take this literally. The barnraising probably demonstrates this ideal most clearly.

Many times the farmer meets with an Amish building contractor and a local lumberyard owner before the fire has stopped steaming. Together they draw up plans to build a new barn. The barn is the largest, most complicated and most expensive of buildings on the Amish homestead.

Clean-Up

Sometimes the clean-up continues for several days, although it is customary to call neighbors together for a day of cleaning up. Often non-Amish neighbors help.

Many times a fire kills some of the livestock. One of the more gruesome tasks in the clean-up is the removal of these animals. Often a tractor-driving neighbor helps remove the cows, horses, mules and calves to be buried in a pit which has been dug in a nearby field.

Disposing of the charred remains, animals, equipment, and manure soaked by the fire engines is difficult and unpleasant.

Soon the wooden beams and steel posts ordered by the contractor arrive. Masonry work must be done to repair walls and foundations. Joists for the second floor are positioned.

Amish neighbors and friends, along with non-Amish friends, come together at dawn. As the sun rises through the morning mists, so a barn will rise from the ashes.

The Barnraising

It is hard to determine who is the boss at a barnraising. The man in charge quietly delegates work to several capable carpenters who keep the other volunteers busy.

Lots of careful behind-the-scenes planning must be done because there isn't time to draw up blueprints and most of the helpers are farmers by occupation instead of builders.

Nothing is prefabricated. The entire structure is built on location. In a single day!

The women participate too. The large number of volunteers requires enormous portions of food. Traditionally there are two snacks taken out to the site, one at mid-morning and one in mid-afternoon. Much of the food is brought by neighbors and friends.

The work halts for the noon meal which normally includes meat, mashed potatoes, lots of vegetables and several desserts and pies. It is important to the family that no one who came to help them in their time of trouble goes away hungry.

Barnraisings are social events for the Amish. Not only does the opportunity to help others provide a break in routine; it serves up a chance to visit with neighbors, relatives, and friends from other districts.

Lively discussions about crops, livestock, milk prices, neighborhood gossip and even a little politics are shared over food or a hammered nail. The sadness brought by fire is gladdened by both the rebuilding of the barn and friendships!

Mutual Aid

The Old Order Amish know they are secure for life, no matter if fire, illness, financial ruin or old age comes. Their community not only disciplines them; it also supports and restores them.

The Amish have traditionally opposed commercial insurance. In Lancaster County they developed an Amish Aid Plan about 1886, and other Amish communities have similar mutual aid plans. Members pay into the fund, either by appraisal or by their ability to pay. A committee makes decisions on disbursements by need.

More and more Amish persons carry commercial insurance these days, especially fire, storm, and liability coverage. But they oppose life insurance adamantly.

The Amish practice private ownership of property. Unlike their Anabaptist cousins, the Hutterites, the Amish do not hold to "complete community of goods." But they believe in "bearing one another's burdens."

Consequently, Amish life is interwoven with constant events geared to helping those among their number who have experienced misfortune (chapter 7 notes Amish efforts to help those beyond their communities) or who could use some help. If a smaller building project is envisioned, an Amishman may call "a frolic," often bringing together six to twelve men to help put up a small horse barn, a shop, a shed, or to help tear down a house or barn elsewhere which is available for its lumber.

Sometimes it's a quilting for a disabled member of a family, sometimes helping a neighbor to butcher, or preparing for a sale. Lots of foods is shared back and forth. Some communities have get-togethers for widows. Others have special occasions for families who have lost children in accidents. Helping to can peaches or filling silo, doing up tomato juice or getting together with one's circle-letter friends—the web of mutual aid constantly surrounds the Amish person.

School boards in Lancaster County have banded together to begin two schools especially designed for handicapped children. Many have noted that the handicapped generally feel less isolated in a community committed to constant mutual aid.

The deacon, as noted earlier, is the person in each church district with special responsibility to oversee day-to-day mutual aid and to monitor the needs of the poor, the widowed, the orphaned, and those disabled by disease and accidents among his district. The system is not perfect, but functions amazingly well for a group which is so reserved about discussing finances openly.

A barn aflame at night is a terrible scene. Before the fire is even extinguished, Amish neighbors are already planning the clean-up and the building of a new barn.

Removing the charred remains, the burnt animals, the twisted equipment, and the manure soaked by the fire engines can be quite difficult and unpleasant.

It is hard to determine who is the boss at a barnraising. The man in charge quietly delegates work to several capable carpenters who keep the other volunteers busy. Most of the helpers are farmers by occupation instead of builders.

Barnraisings are social events for the Amish. Not only does the opportunity to help others provide a break from the routine; it serves up a chance to visit with neighbors, relatives, and friends from other districts. Lively discussions about crops, livestock, milk prices, neighborhood gossip, and even a little politics are shared over food or a hammered nail.

The women participate too. The large number of volunteers requires enormous portions of food. Traditionally there are two snacks taken out to the site, one at mid-morning and one in mid-afternoon. Much of the food is brought by neighbors and friends.

The work halts for the noon meal, which normally includes meat, mashed potatoes, lots of vegetables, and several desserts and pies. It is important to the family that no one who came to help them in their time of trouble should go away hungry.

When the roof goes on, the barnraising is nearly complete. But the Amish community doesn't overlook the family's total needs. Before the unfortunate family can continue with their livelihood, they'll need new livestock, equipment, hay, straw, and feed. Neighbors and relatives help with these needs too.

Struggles and Problems

Yes, the Amish have many problems.

These are not a perfect people. Like all persons who publicly hold up a high standard for themselves, the Amish are expected by general society, and especially their neighbors, to lead exemplary lives. When they fail, it is often considered more of a scandal than if the same failure had surfaced in the life of an average American.

Perfection/Humility

The Amish are not trying to be better than other people in the sense of being superior. But they are trying to be perfect in the sense that Jesus said, "Be ye therefore perfect as I am perfect."

But the Amish also stress the need to be humble before God and fellow humans. Being caught between seeking perfection and seeking humility is one of their biggest problems.

As these people try to be as Christ-like, perfect, and humble as possible, several results surface again and again: 1) a beautiful Christian community takes root and thrives as a living example of redeemed humankind; 2) the dual themes of perfection and humility provide fertile ground for many to grow and blossom; 3) for some, the tension is too great, and they suffer emotional and spiritual anguish.

Those in anguish often take one of two approaches: a) they deny their feelings, resulting in unhappiness and even mental illness; or b) more commonly, they leave the group, either to form a new "perfect" community, or to become more flamboyant and join the mainstream "imperfect" society.

This stress on perfection and humility has been both an asset and a weakness for the Amish. It has brought into being some of the most unusual and beautiful Christian communities in all history; it has also resulted in a multitude of church splits, self-righteousness, and unhealthy rebellion and rejection.

The central problem facing Amish society is easy enough to understand—how to hold this unique community of faith together without crushing the individual identities of its members. Leaders try to find the way. Sometimes it's rather difficult.

Mental Health

Studies have shown that the pressures of Amish communal society can bring considerable mental anguish into the lives of some. By the same token, the security and sense of belonging decreases mental turmoil for many others. Most observers agree, therefore, that the number of cases of mental illness among the Amish approximates the national average.

Pressure for Youth

Youth, for teenagers everywhere, is a time of identity search. Similarly, Amish young people many times face a great deal of tension as they decide whether to stay or to leave the world that nurtured them. Many young people sample the "freedom" of the larger world after they turn sixteen and are permitted to "run around."

Much has been written about the rowdiness of some Amish young people. Noisy gatherings and drinking parties are not condoned by parents and church leaders, and many Amish young people also frown on these practices. But nevertheless, some Amish youth do express a great deal of rebellious behavior during these years.

It has been observed that those who've already decided to leave the Amish may be less inclined to rowdiness than those who are sitting on the fence. It is also true that many times those who test the boundaries the hardest often emerge as leaders in the Amish community later.

The pressure builds up steam until the decision is made. Many young people do leave. But many more stay. Some even leave and then return. In Lancaster County, Amish leaders believe that more young people are staying with the church in recent years, perhaps as many as eighty percent.

Bundling

A controversial courtship practice dating from medieval and colonial American times, called bundling, is still allowed by many Amish communities. Sometimes known as "bed courtship," a young man, supposedly fully clad, visits with his girlfriend, also fully clothed, in bed.

In some settings, this folk tradition may be harmless, even beautiful. In many others, however, it has led to a serious decline in morals. Many pre-marital pregnancies have resulted. Few issues have caused so much anguish and division among the Amish.

Shunning

Perhaps the hardest aspect of Amish life is shunning.

The Amish believe that if a member has violated his or her baptismal vows, fallen into sin, or gone against the rules and regulations of the group, and has refused to heed the counsel and concern of the fellowship, that member must be excommunicated. In its purest form, excommunication, for all Christian groups, simply declares the reality—"You have, by your actions, taken yourself outside our fellowship."

The practice of shunning adds social avoidance to the excommunication. In essence, shunning requires members to cease social and business relationships with the person shunned. Many believe this means they cannot eat at the same table or take anything directly from the hand of the shunned person.

Practices vary a great deal from group to group and from family to family. In some cases, shunning is for life, in others, only for a period of years. In some groups, the practice is severe, even harsh, and has led to great bitterness. In others, the spirit of the rule is maintained rather than the letter of the rule.

For leaders who debate how severe excommunication should be, the point of the practice remains central: the hope is that the erring member will repent and return to the fellowship. This often happens. But many times the discipline overwhelms the one disciplined, and rejection of the Amish way results.

Most Amish believe that, in spite of its potential unpleasantness, shunning in its various forms contributes in a positive way to the unity and purity of their church.

Physical danger surrounds an Amish family. The farm is known as one of the more dangerous atmospheres. The highway often becomes a hostile, even deadly setting. The Amish, who choose the simple and the small over the large and the mighty, can easily seem belittled and bewildered in the modern world.

The Amish are not trying to be better than other people in the sense of being superior. But being caught between seeking perfection and seeking humility has become both an asset and a weakness of their way of life. (Note the umbrella above, the color of the buggy from New Wilmington, Pa., below.)

A people who choose to be deliberately different have to distinguish between persecution (unfair harassment from others or the government because of their beliefs), trouble (unfortunate circumstances anyone may suffer such as cancer or a flooded field) and stubbornness (an unmerited inflexibility, even an unbending paranoia). Many Amish are adept to discern these differences; on the other hand, some "suffer righteously" for problems they bring on themselves!

Fires bring trouble. Sometimes the victims are Amish, and others help them. Sometimes the Amish, like this young firefighter above, are the ones who help non-Amish victims.

Sometimes Amish society seems lost in a blizzard, frozen in inflexible rules that oppress the young who turn their backs and slip away before the leaders understand what's happening.

Compassionate but firm leadership remains crucial to the survival of the Amish way.

When home no longer seems warm, when the ice covers all and the sunshine of love has fled into the distance, young people will leave. Home is the nest of Amish society.

Harvest Time

In the end, the harvest always comes. The Amish know this, and shape their whole lives accordingly. The seasons of the Amish way embrace the reaping as much as the sowing. Harvest will come.

Joy of Harvest

Few events on a farm bring as much pleasure as the reaping of a good crop. An uncultivated planting brings one of the earliest yields in April—dandelions. Soon the garden offers up strawberries and peas. Then comes the first cutting of alfalfa.

Ripened wheat remains one of the most picturesque of all harvests. Technologies vary from community to community, but the sheaves of wheat, cut and lying neatly across the stubble, create a joyous feeling.

Harvest takes hard work, to be sure. Threshing is undoubtedly one of the more wearing of farm chores. But to see the fruit of the soil brings much joy.

Hay and alfalfa are normally harvested several times a year. Tobacco cutting time arrives in August and September. Potato harvest is followed by the bringing in of the corn. And when the corn is in, the weddings begin!

Bad Years

Farming brings with it many risks. Some years the earth is dry. The crops wither. The stunted harvest leaves the corncrib half empty. Other times it is too wet and the crops rot from moisture.

The restrictions Amish farmers place upon themselves make it more difficult to harness nature's quirks. But one can accept failed crops more easily. And if a neighbor farmer with a big tractor is able to get all of his hay in before the rain comes, while the Amish farmer with his small horse-drawn operation fails to beat the rain, then again the Amish farmer takes comfort in the values he has accepted.

Wheat harvest requires hard work. But the beauty of seeing the bounty of the earth brings great joy. Harvest time is a theme central to the Amish wholeness.

One Amish farmer observed that a great advantage to him in not having a radio is that he's not constantly worrying about the weather. "I don't have the wits scared out of me every time a cloud comes up!" he laughed.

Hard times do come. The Amish way does not guarantee a prosperous harvest. But the Amish community, in sharing freely with each other, blunts the disaster of a failed harvest.

Harvest of Life

The Amish do tend to "retire" early, and yet they never retire. Older persons do everything they can to help the younger generation get a start. This includes the common practice of giving up one's vocation (in farming or business) early, so the sons and daughters can raise their own families in a world in which they as young parents are primarily responsible. An Amish father may step aside in his late forties, assisting his son as needed, but he may also start a second job.

Some of these second vocations are on the homeplace. Rebuilding pieces of farm equipment, repairing shoes, selling hardware, making furniture, growing extra vegetables for market—on and on the list goes. Many times this second vocation is less exhausting than farming, and can be tailored to fit the energies of the older man as he slows down. Thus he, in effect, may never fully retire in the sense of ceasing to perform meaningful work.

The same is true for the Amish woman. As long as she is physically able, she continues to quilt and cook and garden and visit others.

Husband and Wife

Husband and wife in Amish society have an interesting relationship. Much has been made of the patriarchal nature of the Amish home. This is true, in the sense that the man goes ahead, officially.

But in fact, these men and women experience more partnership and comradeship in their relationships than most modern Americans. On the farm, the husband and wife labor side by side, take most meals together, and visit with each other constantly throughout the day. This comradeship especially emerges in their elder years.

Joining

Does anyone who is not born into an Amish family ever become a member of the Amish faith?

Yes. It is very difficult, because faith for the Amish is more than saying words or signing a paper; it envelops the whole of life, every aspect of one's identity from cradle to grave. It is a big step.

The Old Order Amish do not actively participate in mission programs designed to attract persons to their faith. But the witness of their lives and their faith has touched millions.

Numerous persons have attempted to join the Old Order Amish. Some found the transition too traumatic. Others, however, have found in the Amish church the Christian fellowship for which they have been searching. One of the leading historians among the Amish is a young man who grew up Catholic, went to the University of Notre Dame, became acquainted with the Old Order Amish, joined the church, later married an Amish girl, and has lived with his adopted people for many years.

The Amish Harvest

Belonging to a people is a precious thing.

Keeping the Amish communities dynamic without letting them come apart at the seams requires tremendous effort, discipline, sacrifice, and faith in God. Limits must be shaped without losing the joy of life.

In the end, the harvest always comes. What was sown will bear fruit. The Amish people, on the average, are probably some of the most fulfilled and contented human beings in our world today.

Hard times do come. The Amish way does not guarantee a prosperous harvest. But the Amish community, in sharing freely with each other, blunts the disaster of a failed harvest.

Belonging to a people is a precious thing. Keeping the Amish communities dynamic without letting them come apart at the seams requires tremendous effort, discipline, sacrifice, and faith in God. Limits must be shaped without losing the joy of the harvest.

The grandparents house often takes the form of an extension to the main house. The Amish tend to "retire" early, yet they never fully retire. A second vocation often provides a way for older folks to make a meaningful contribution until the day they die.

The Amish people, on the average, are probably some of the most fulfilled and contented human beings in our world today.

Readings and Sources

General Introductions

Denlinger, A. Martha. **Real People.** Herald Press, Scottdale, Pennsylvania, 1975.

Good, Merle and Phyllis. **Twenty Most Asked Questions about the Amish and Mennonites.** Good Books, Intercourse, Pennsylvania, 1979.

Hostetler, John A. **Amish Life.** Herald Press, Scottdale, Pennsylvania, 1952.

Miller, Levi. **Our People: The Amish and Mennonites of Ohio.** Herald Press, Scottdale, Pennsylvania, 1983.

Beliefs, History, and Lifestyle

Bender, H. S. **Anabaptist Vision.** Herald Press, Scottdale, Pennsylvania, 1944.

Braght, Thieleman J. van, Comp. **Martyrs Mirror.** Herald Press, Scottdale, Pennsylvania, 1950.

Devoted Christian's Prayerbook. Pathway Publishing Corp., LaGrange, Indiana, 1984.

Dortrecht Confession of Faith. Pathway Publishing Corp., LaGrange, Indiana.

Dyck, Cornelius, J. **An Introduction to Mennonite History.** Herald Press, Scottdale, Pennsylvania, 1967.

Fisher, Gideon L. **Farm Life and Its Changes.** Pequea Publishers, Gordonville, Pennsylvania, 1978.

Gingerich, Orland. **The Amish of Canada.** Herald Press, Scottdale, Pennsylvania, 1972.

Hostetler, John A. **Amish Society.** Johns Hopkins University Press, Baltimore, Maryland, 1968.

Ruth, John L. **A Quiet and Peaceable Life.** Good Books, Intercourse, Pennsylvania, 1979.

Scott, Stephen. **Plain Buggies.** Good Books, Intercourse, Pennsylvania, 1981.

_____ . **Why Do They Dress That Way?** Good Books, Intercourse, Pennsylvania, 1985.

Amish Schools

Fisher, Sara and Rachel Stahl. **The Amish School.** Good Books, Intercourse, Pennsylvania, 1985.

Hostetler, John A. and Gertrude E. Huntingdon. **Children in Amish Society.** Holt, Rinehart and Winston, Inc., New York, New York, 1971.

Keim, Albert N. **Compulsory Education and the Amish.** Beacon Press, Boston, Massachusetts, 1975.

Fiction

DeAngeli, Marguerite. **Henner's Lydia.** Doubleday, New York, New York, 1937.

_____ . **Yonie Wondernose.** Doubleday, New York, New York, 1944.

Good, Merle and Erika Stone. **Nicole Visits an Amish Farm.** Walker & Company, New York, New York, 1982.

Smucker, Barbara. **Amish Adventure.** Herald Press, Scottdale, Pennsylvania, 1983.

Yoder, Joseph W. **Rosanna of the Amish.** Herald Press, Scottdale, Pennsylvania, 1973.

Music

Verlag von den Amischen Gemeinden in Lancaster County, Pennsylvania. **Ausbund.**

_____ . **Unpartheyisches Gesangbuch.**

Cookbooks

Good, Phyllis Pellman. **Cooking and Memories.** Good Books, Intercourse, Pennsylvania, 1983.

Good, Phyllis Pellman and Rachel Thomas Pellman. **From Amish and Mennonite Kitchens.** Good Books, Intercourse, Pennsylvania, 1984.

Miller, Mark Eric. **Amish Cooking.** Herald Press, Scottdale, Pennsylvania, 1980.

Quilts

Bishop, Robert and Elizabeth Safanda. **A Gallery of Amish Quilts.** E. P. Dutton and Compay, Inc., New York, New York, 1976.

Haders, Phyllis. **Sunshine and Shadow: The Amish and Their Quilts.** Universe Books, New York, New York, 1976.

Horton, Roberta. **Amish Adventure.** C & T Publishing, Lafayette, California, 1983.

Lawson, Suzy. **Amish Inspirations.** Amity Publications, Cottage Grove, Oregon, 1982.

Pellman, Rachel T. **Amish Quilt Patterns.** Good Books, Intercourse, Pennsylvania, 1984.

Pellman, Rachel and Kenneth. **The World of Amish Quilts.** Good Books, Intercourse, Pennsylvania, 1984.

Pottinger, David. **Quilts from the Indiana Amish.** E. P. Dutton, Inc., New York, New York, 1983.

Periodicals

Blackboard Bulletin. Amish periodical published monthly. Pathway Publishing House, Aylmer, Ontario.

Budget, The. Sugarcreek, Ohio, 1890. A weekly newspaper serving the Amish and Mennonite communities.

Diary, The. A church newsletter serving the Old Order Society. Pequea Publishers, Gordonville, Pennsylvania.

Family Life. Amish periodical published monthly. Pathway Publishing House, Aylmer, Ontario.

Young Companion. Amish periodical published monthly. Pathway Publishing House, Aylmer, Ontario.